Meditate Your Stress Away

10 Steps to Stay Calm in Times of Unease, maintain a State of Happiness Throughout a Busy Lifestyle, and Be More Aware of Your Inner Tranquility

Odette Herald

ISBN: 979-8-6663-6899-2

CONTENTS

Introduction

I remember the day I decided to give meditation a try. I felt silly and foolish lighting my candles, setting serene music, sitting crisscross applesauce on a large pillow, imitating what I'd seen in countless movies, and hoping no one would come barging in with a video camera. I'll admit, the whole thing felt silly. I honestly don't think that attempt really had any effects on my psyche like I expected.

But I had many friends who made meditation a daily habit and swore by it. So, I showed up the next day and tried again. And I felt…. nothing. "Bored" would be the term that comes to mind. But the more I tried and failed, the more interest I took into why I was failing, and the more I started to do research on the proper ways to meditate and the expected outcomes to watch for.

I came back to it, day after day. It only took me about a month before I started really looking forward to my meditation time. Then I realized what it was doing to me. It was my short period of my day dedicated to quieting the storm in my head. My mind is constantly focused on about 10 different things at once, so being able to stop and Clear it felt entirely refreshing.

I came to realize that the actual effects of meditation were taking place outside of my allotted practice time. I started recognizing that whatever obstacles were thrown at me during my day, meditation was arming me against overwhelm. As time went on I saw more and more results.

Giving our heads that needed break arms us against the daily storm of stressful hurdles. And we begin to understand that we get to choose not to let them affect us. This is what meditation does. It gives us our armor to kick ass at life.

So why doesn't everyone meditate if there are such profound and lasting results?

Just the idea of meditation can seem intimidating to people, leaving them scared even to try meditation. Most of us believe we don't have time to fit it in to our overwhelmingly busy lives. There are also those who prioritize working out and eating healthy—but who really thinks about having to take care of our mind?

Living in today's world, more people are anxious and overwhelmed than ever. This leads to reduce energy, gets us sick, and makes us cranky, which makes us have less time to do the plethora of tasks we need to get done, which leads to more stress and anxiety—the circle never stops. No wonder we don't think we have time to add a meditation practice to our day.

What most don't realize is that meditation is the key to stopping this circle from continuing. And it only takes five minutes a day. Meditation is that break in our day to stop our minds and to give it a rest. The brain needs this as much as our bodies need nutrition. Meditation helps us gain back our concentration, dedication, tranquility, vitality, optimism, serenity, composure, rejuvenation, satisfaction, empathy, tranquility, persistence, and perseverance. The list of benefits meditation has to our daily lives goes on and on. And we don't even have to dedicate that much time to it!

As you will learn, there are many meditation approaches, hundreds of different methods, and tips. Try as many as you'd like and choose the path that works best for you. Mix it up when you want and keep coming back. Add a meditation practice to your daily routine and in time you will be armed with all of the clarity necessary to live your most tranquil life possible.

Chapter 1: Your Busy Schedule

Most people don't realize the benefits meditation can have on their lives. Human beings are understandably stressed, particularly in today's world with a multitude of demanding events, from busy schedules and social pressures, to diseases and now pandemics. Thanks to the multitude of existing stressors, we must be armed with the knowledge required to be emotionally healthy enough to control what we let affect us.

Many aren't aware that meditating for only a short time every day can have an extremely powerful impact on our lives. Meditation has been shown to help relieve stress, strengthen focus, build confidence, handle difficult circumstances with ease, and increase positivity.

Studies have even shown that the negative effects of stress, anxiety, and depression have been alleviated when people meditate daily. Add a meditation routine to your repertoire and live a calmer, satisfied, and more fulfilled life as a result.

Life can be dynamic, effortless, and beautiful if we choose it to be. Meditation brings awareness to each moment and understanding that we can be grateful for each triumph and each hiccup that comes along. This builds our insight, our outlook on life, our imagination, and our contentment. It also helps us to have more compassion for others. When we can get creative about why each of our own experiences benefits us, this opens our minds to understand why others' actions can also be crucial, which builds insight, and a profound sense of our true meaning.

The ability to master our thoughts is part of fulfilling our goals and desires. By relaxing the mind, we will achieve this self-mastery and begin modifying and removing our negative or unwanted thoughts. A change in our way of thinking aligns our energies with the vibrations of universal energy, and we begin to see meaningful changes and progress in all aspects of our lives.

A lot of people who haven't tried meditation are concerned that meditation might be boring. But the thing about meditation is that it is just a way for your mind to relax. Think about how tense our bodies get when we are stressed or overworked. All our bodies need is a nice stretch to relieve the tension. Our minds go through the same rigors, and It's just as important to ensure your mind is getting a good stretch to relieve tension as well your body. That is exactly what meditation does. Once you start a meditation practice, you'll come to understand how very soothing and gratifying this part of your day is.

Meditation improves focus. Once you hone your meditation practice, you will notice how effortlessly you will be able to concentrate on a task, without worrying about all of the things surrounding you that would have once distracted you. This will increase your productivity dramatically.

Meditation helps you solve problems, sans stress. Sitting quietly and focusing on a problem during meditation is extremely different than trying to focus on the same problem while running around and doing your errands, while at work, or while driving and trying to simultaneously concentrate on traffic.

Meditation eliminates stress almost immediately as soon as you begin to practice it; this is because your whole mind is cleared of negative thoughts during meditation by concentrating on your breathe or an affirmation. Often during meditation, you can even sense the healing process.

Meditation encourages patience. After you meditate for a while, you will start to notice that the rest of the time you aren't meditating, you can handle any situation easier. This is because meditation offers you the chance to step back from life around you and is akin to pressing the restart button. When faced with an obstacle, you'll be armed with breath and tranquility—which is the worthy opponent to life's hurdles.

Meditation gives you peace. People who meditate are often happy. The world looks more beautiful because you now are more aware of each moment. When we are trained to focus on the moment and the beauty and lesson it has to offer us, our world becomes a brighter place to be.

Meditation frees the mind from negativity. Being able to see the world for its beauty also means being able to view what might have once appeared as a challenging situation with ease and optimism. When you build inner harmony, it starts to radiate and shine from inside of you.

Meditation eradicates negative feelings. Your mind is cleared of negative thoughts during meditation because you are focusing on only positive thoughts. The less you concentrate on negative thoughts, the less you feel negative emotions. Your mind simply can't concentrate on two opposing emotions at the same time. When you focus on positive emotions, negative ones can't affect you.

Meditation helps you seek out positive people. When you recognize your own inner positive emotions, an amazing thing starts to happen with those around you. You will slowly start to notice that you can pick up on others' emotions, whether they are good or bad. And the more you choose to gravitate toward those who are more positive, the happier you are in turn.

Meditation grounds you. This is a huge benefit. The more you meditate, the more aware you are about your surroundings and the feelings that are associated with them. This strengthens your connection to the world. It boosts your appreciation. It helps you relate to other people, animals, and nature. This can greatly impact the way you act towards everything around you in a more positive, high-energy way.

Meditation increases your awareness. When you meditate, you begin to see the true colors of life. You see more abundance than absence; you believe that the world is in balance rather than in disorder.

You communicate with the universe when you meditate. This is one of the most profound benefits of meditation. Call it what you'd like: the supreme being, god, the universe, mother nature, you will have an entirely profound experience with meditation (and with life) when you trust that there is a higher power out there that is completely in love with you and just wants you to get over your fears and become the best person you can possibly be.

This will greatly increase your meditation results as well. If you have a problem and seek a solution, ask the universe your question, and wait in expectant giddiness for the answer. The answer will reveal itself when and how it wants, so don't get discouraged if you don't find an obvious answer the first time you sit down and ask your question. Eventually you will get the answer you seek. This is where words like coincidence and intuition come onto the playing field. When you ask the universe a question, it will answer in the way it wants you to receive it. It is up to you to be open enough to receive it, and meditation greatly increases your senses to recognize the message.

Meditation breaks down obstacles. What are your truest wishes? What do you see yourself doing that you are too scared to do or even share? How do you wish you could give back to the world? When you meditate, it breaks down your barriers to view your truest self. It also raises your confidence to be able to view your obstacles in a simpler light.

Over time the most difficult task will have the simplest solution. This is your Eureka moment! The moment you have quieted your mind enough to be able to look at a seemingly difficult situation in a new light and realize that it has the simplest solution. This is because you have quieted negative feelings, strengthened positive ones, simplified your thoughts, and eliminated conflict.

Meditation increases your energy. Because you have turned into an optimistic, peaceful, intuitive machine, you will be able to live out each day feeling into your high energy emotions. You can make each decision with the understanding of what each outcome will bring you and those around you. You will the aspiration to take care of others, because when we give to others, we are at our highest energy, and we benefit the greatest.

Meditation is extremely convenient. You can meditate for as little as five minutes when you first wake up or just before you go to sleep, while waiting at the Dr.'s office, in the shower or bath, while on hold with your cable company, during a boring meeting, while standing in line at H&M, on a plane, or on a train. It is so incredibly convenient, it's a small wonder everyone isn't incorporating a meditation practice into their lives. The options are limitless.

Individuals of all ages and backgrounds can benefit from adding meditation to their daily routines. Today, meditation is a global trend that is vital for everyone to endure the rigors of our increasingly complex world.

Chapter 2: The Colorful World of Meditation

Different meditation techniques have different objectives and employ a range of techniques. To decide which technique is right for you, start by thinking about what you want from a meditation practice and how much time you would like to spend doing it. You can start with five minutes a day, and if that's all you'd like to spend going forward that is completely up to you. Or you can gradually increase your time and find your meditation sweet spot: the perfect amount of time that makes you feel like you've practiced enough, balanced with the amount of free time you have in each day. You can also break your practice up and meditate twice a day. This is great when you'd like to start and end your day meditating, as both times of the day have different intentions.

In practically all cultures, various meditative practices are known by many names, but finding one that works for you is easy. The following are just a few of the more popular meditations and can be used individually, together or in conjunction with any specific meditation practice you may currently enjoy.

Focus Meditation

The earliest record of meditation is from India in its Hindu scriptures called *Tantras*. In the Tantras, the meditation practice called *Nyasa* was written. Nyasa meditation is a focus meditation, where hymns or specific idols are imagined in different parts of the body. One popular idol to focus on is light. When sitting and closing your eyes, focus first on your feet and imagine them filling with a golden warm light. Then imagine your legs slowly being filled with light as well. Slowly continue to feel your body being filled up with this light to the top of your head. Breathe this light in and then out into the world. Repeat throughout the practice.

Standing Meditation

This meditation means Standing Like a Tree. Start by rooting your feet, either touching sole-to-toe or standing hip-width apart. Rest your arms at your sides or place your hands in front of your chest, palms touching as if in prayer, but your fingers separated. Stand up straight, but don't be rigid. Relax everything else. You can either have your eyes closed, or open and concentrating on something pleasant in front of you, such as your favorite painting, or a blank wall. Just make sure you're not watching something on tv— Desperate Housewives of Atlanta won't lead anyone down a path of tranquility. Focus on releasing the tension from your mind and your body. You can imagine you are a giant tree in a beautiful meadow on a gorgeous day.

The River

Imagine you are standing in a stream that is knee-height. The water is the perfect temperature. There is the slightest current. Your hands are at your sides, swaying in the slight current of the water. Imagine the slightest breeze on your face and in your hair.

The focus of this is separating yourself from your current situation and imagining that you are really in this beautiful, peaceful stream. It calms your mind and separates you from past stressful or unsavory situations. It helps you realize that those situations aren't what make you who you are. That you are in control of your own outcome.

Meditation in Motion

If you are one who doesn't like to be still, Tai Chi, various methods of Qigong, and yoga are fluid forms of meditation. It is an excellent way to still the mind while being in motion and it creates a strong, flexible, and healthy body.

In comparison to other types of meditation, anyone who performs Tai Chi, Qigong, or yoga will make greater progress on their path to living their true, constant state of tranquility and happiness because they are strengthening their body at the same time.

There are currently many ways to find a great instructor for any one of these types of exercise-meditations. The best way would be to go to instructor-led classes. You can also find apps and online classes if you are looking for a more flexible or less expensive route. For yoga I personally have *Yogaglo* which I absolutely love since I can choose my instructor, length of time, and area of focus every single time I work out in the comfort of my own home. And I find the daily combination of yoga and meditation particularly healing for every aspect of my life. This combination took me awhile to find, so experimenting with the different meditation types is fun and will lead you to find the path that is right for you.

Centering Meditation

Centering meditation is focusing on the present moment to take your mind away from negative emotions. This practice originated in the Aikido – a martial art technique the Japanese use in order to be in transcendent harmonization with the world and nature. It's used to train your mind to stay calm during the time away from meditation in order to handle adverse situations calmly and not let them affect you as much as they might normally. If you feel overwhelmed, anxious, stressed, scatterbrained, tired, unfocused or edgy, grounding meditation can help you focus on your "core" or the very center of your body.

The body's center is not the same for everyone and is the location you feel centered at when you look inward. This may be just behind your bellybutton, where your third eye is located, your brain, or your heart. The more you focus on staying centered during your meditation, the more you'll be able to train yourself to stay grounded outside of meditation, which is great for diffusing difficult situations and remaining stress-free.

When practicing a centering meditation, the idea is to locate your center, focus on it, and while you breathe in, imagine lightness and bright, positive energy being pulled into your center. As you exhale, imagine all your negative feelings flowing out of you from your core, out of your body and out to the world. Then repeat throughout your entire practice.

Doing this exercise on a regular basis makes us more aware of our center. The importance of this is to make us sturdier and more grounded, and the more grounded we are, the more things roll off our shoulders, and the less stressful situations will bother us. Basically, we can handle practically anything.

Walking Meditation

This is a great meditation to utilize when we find it difficult to sit in one place, or if we've dedicated an allotted time to meditate, but it's gorgeous outside and we don't want to be stuck inside. Walking meditation is exactly as the name implies: you're walking as you mediate. What's the difference between walking and a walking meditation?

Walking meditation is the act of intentionally noticing your breathing and the senses around you. What do you normally think about when you go for a stroll? Do you think about what to cook for dinner, or who you can call so you're not walking alone? Are you waiting for your dog to go to the bathroom already so you can go inside to continue watching you show?

When you meditate while walking, your intention is to notice your breathing. Breathe in slowly and fill up your entire lungs. Then breathe out to expel negative thoughts out and away from you. Focus on your senses around you. What does the air feel like on your skin? How does the breeze feel on your clothes and in your hair? How does the sun feel? What can you smell? Can you smell the moss on the trees? The grass? The hotdog stand? What can you hear? Are there birds chirping? The sound of the trees swaying in the breeze? Are there waves crashing on the shore? Pay attention to how you are walking. Are you relaxing your shoulders? Are you walking too fast to notice much? Is your entire body tense? Relax your body as well as your mind to get the physical benefits as an added bonus.

This practice is much more soothing than regular walking, because you are focusing on the moment and taking your thoughts away from the things that might make you anxious, stress, or tired because your brain is on overdrive from thinking too much. This relaxes your mind and makes you more aware of the things occurring right now that can make your more serene. Doing this practice often (just like with the other meditation methods) builds and fortifies our capability to be in the moment, and be tranquil during the rest of our day.

Mantra Meditation

This practice is an easy and yet powerful meditation, capable of calming your mind and connecting you to your inner spirit. It uses a mantra as a focal point. A mantra is a word or sentence with the ability to transfer us into a deeper, more peaceful consciousness. For this practice, the mantra most widely used is "Om." This is originally from Hinduism and is pronounced as "Aum." The three syllables are each utilized, and each have their own importance in traditional Hinduism. The beginning (the "Ah" sound) represents your foundation as it focuses on the creation, or beginning, of life. The middle ("Uh" sound) represents our self-preservation, and the "mmm" sound at the end represents freeing yourself from any negative energies. Focusing on these three objectives during the chant connects your mind to your intentions. The point of this is to connect ourselves to our natural surroundings.

The amazing thing about this practice is that the "Om" sound causes a vibration starting from the diaphragm extending through your body and out to the air around you. Doing this practice starts a vibration, and the frequency that we vibrate at is actually the same frequency that that is found in everything in nature, which is 432 Hz. This entire practice is set with the intention that we are becoming more aligned and at one with nature.

Relaxation meditation

When you want to relax, research suggests that the physical calming results from the relaxation method can be activated in several ways, including sitting in a cross-legged position, lying down, keeping your eyes closed, or open and focusing on an object such as a lit candle. Soothing music is also widely popular. Then focus on clearing your mind from any thoughts. This can be hard to do when first starting a meditation practice.

You can use focus techniques such as focusing on your third eye, focusing on the dark inside your closed eyelids, or concentrating on a pleasant object in the room, such as a lit candle. Because of the close relationship between the mind and the body, the more often you meditate, the more relaxed the mind becomes, the greater the state of relaxation for the body.

Contemplation meditation

Contemplation meditation is one of the leading types of meditation. It has its own distinct and unique impact on body and mind. This can be used when we are stressed about a certain situation and are unsure as to what to do. You can sit comfortably and close your eyes in a peaceful room much like the relaxation meditation.

First, focus on a challenge you are faced with. Really spend a moment thinking about and visualizing it in detail. Next, release the question into the universe and focus on being quiet during the remaining time of your meditation and see if a solution pops into your head.

The answer can be produced the very first time you meditate on your question, or it can come around the 20th time. It can also happen outside of your meditation when you least expect it, and in a form you wouldn't expect. The point here is to keep coming back, and eventually you will get the answer you are looking for.

Chapter 3: Choosing the Right Practice

The majority of meditation experts out there suggest you meditate about ten to twenty minutes in the morning and before bed. But if you want to stick with it, start out small and build up to your ideal time. Also, we are all so delightfully different from one another, it is important to stick with what works for you, not what others might be doing or what you think you're supposed to be doing.

You can find the time during the day for a longer meditation, or sneak in mini meditations throughout the day. Don't give up because you think you have to practice for long periods of time. The gloriousness of meditation is that everyone finds their own perfect amount of time and place that is right for them.

There are so many ways to meditate, so one of the most important things I want to say is that if you are new to meditation, there are no rules other than relax! Meditation is not work or a contest. It is a way to find your own benefits that you are seeking.

There is no one way you have to sit or stand to meditate. Don't limit yourself to just one type if you don't want to. You don't have to even sit. Like we've learned in the previous chapter, we can meditate while we sit, stand, walk, or while doing soothing movements. You can even lay down if you'd like. Just take note if you keep falling asleep, as this would not make your meditation beneficial.

How you meditate is likely to depend on your goal. I change the way I meditate depending on what I want my meditation practice to achieve. When I am nervous, I prefer to focus on my breathing or to calm my body consciously. When I've got too much in my head that I have been thinking about, I like to close my eyes and look at the darkness behind them and focus on not thinking of anything.

If I have a goal that I am overwhelmed about, I like to just focus on it and let my mind rest from working to solve the problem. In fact, a lot of people use this method as a way to solve a problem. They ask their specific question at the beginning of meditation, let their thoughts rest, and then they can clearly see the path to their end goal. I have done this many times, and although no little ferry is inside my thoughts telling me any specific answer, I do find my views less tangled and therefore can draw a better plan to a goal.

Think of meditation as your fixer. It helps you get to your goals, whether that is to find a solution to a difficult problem, or to feel calmer, or to be more mindful.

Chapter 4: Location, Location, Location

Choose a location to meditate. Where do you feel is most soothing, comforting, quiet place? The area for you that is most tranquil that you can have to yourself for at least five minutes every day is your ideal meditation location. Make sure you have something comfortable to lay or sit on, is set to a comfortable temperature, and feels tranquil. This could be a park bench, your tub, your couch, your study, your linen closet. Just make sure it is calming to you and that you'll be able to set up any added objects you'd like to heighten your meditation experience with (such as candles, music, blankets, etc.)

Most of the meditations can be done at the location of

your choosing, although I might not encourage laying down on a park bench if you'd rather not have people stare at you, or do your tai chi in your office if it's a professional atmosphere. You can mix it up. You get to be the one to choose which type you'd like to do and where to do it. Just remember what your intention is. It's probably best not to lie down to meditate if you repeatedly fall asleep. And if you tend to be a person who is uncomfortable sitting, you have the choice not to sit. Go on a meditation walk or try out a moving meditation.

The world of meditation is so deliciously versatile that I encourage everyone to try as many types as they'd like in as many locations as they'd like. Mixing up where you do your meditations and which types you choose to practice can also keep your routine fun and interesting; kind of like when you've been dating the same person for a while and you want to mix it up to keep the relationship fun—you can do the same with meditation. You don't have to limit yourself as soon as you've found a practice you like. You may like more than one practice, and you never know until you try.

Here are a few locations to get your creative juices flowing.

In your home

This is where the majority of meditation practice takes place. Meditation can be such an intimate experience, it's no wonder most people prefer to practice in the comfort of their own home. With the importance of being relaxed while meditating, doing so in your home—where we are usually the most secure—makes a lot of sense.

Choose the location that speaks best to you as the most tranquil, soothing, and positive. This can be on your patio, on your bed, on a yoga mat or cushion on the floor, your couch, or anywhere you feel is the place you are most peaceful.

Make sure this is a place where you can get some alone time and some quiet. If you choose to meditate on your couch but your family is watching a movie, you won't really be able to have 100% of your intentions focused on meditation. It's also not a bad idea to just let your family know that you are in "do-not-disturb" mode for the next few minutes, so they know they are unauthorized to interrupt your practice. Hopefully, they listen.

At the park

You can practice pretty much all the meditation types at the park. I like the park because it's usually free (bonus!) It's scenic which helps set the scene for tranquility, and it's a great excuse to be outdoors, away from traffic, your house, your job, and all your other tasks.

Physically stepping out of your normal route to go to the park helps take you away from all of your other tasks that need to get done, as well as separates you from objects that can set your mind running when familiar things you look at tend to trigger your memory of stressful things.

This is a great place to focus on the senses, how your body is feeling, and ease your mind from any wayward thoughts that might creep up. You can sit on a park bench, bring a picnic blanket and sit on the grass, walk around, or practice your moving meditations.

Even if you designate your home as the place you normally meditate, you can mix it up and go to the park—especially if it's a beautiful day outside and you're looking out your window wishing you were out there.

In the steam room at the gym

This is an excellent place for your sitting and laying meditations. The steam room is a physically cleansing place: the act of steaming excretes toxins from your body by making you sweat. So, adding a mental cleanse to your steam room moment takes your experience to the next level.

While sitting or laying (if room permits) in the steam room, close your eyes and set your intentions. You can also ask a question and sit in intentional quiet to receive an answer. Or if your head is on overload, you can focus on clearing your mind and spending the time thinking of nothing. All of these are great ways to *mentally* excrete your toxins while you are *physically* excreting your toxins. And then, you know, go take a shower!

In your car before you turn on the engine

Meditating before you go hit the road—especially if you have a long drive ahead of you filled with traffic—can set your intention to drive peacefully. It's much better than waking up, getting ready, running out of your house, and just hitting the road.

Taking that break just before we drive helps us to stop and be in the moment, and not stuck thinking about what you have to do at work, and then at home, and how long this drive is going to last, and how much you don't like driving, etc.

The next time you need to leave for work, get out to your car a few minutes before you have to, sit in your seat, play some soft music if you'd like, close your eyes, and clear your mind. Then when you're done, turn on the engine, ease out of the driveway, and experience one of the most peaceful drives you've ever had. The more you do this, the harder it will be to get upset at the person who just cut you off.

On your bed

This is personally my go-to spot. It's comfy, fluffy, and it usually means I get to go to bed soon, or It's a great excuse for me to keep staying in bed after my alarm has gone off in the morning.

Waking up and meditating right off the bat is one of

the most glorious ways to get up, and it sets a positive intention for the day.

After your alarm goes off, turn it off, and either meditate while lying in the same position, or sit up and cross your legs with your blanket still wrapped around you if you'd like. This is such a great feeling since your mind is in that delicious stage of still waking, that doing something this beneficial—and, come on, *easy*—will start your day off right. And any obstacles that come your way throughout the day will slowly become effortless.

I also enjoy meditating on my bed at the end of my day, just before bed. Jumping onto my bed in my pajamas, face washed and teeth brushed helps me know that I'm ending my day right. It also cleanses my mind of any challenges I might have encountered throughout my day.

Have you ever crawled into bed completely exhausted, turned off the light, and closed your eyes—only to find your mind racing with a bunch of random thoughts? Meditating at the end of the day helps clear your mind of that, so you can go to bed with your *mind* rested as well as your body.

At your desk at work

This is a great location for the more subtle meditations that you can do on one of your breaks. All you have to do is sit in your office chair and close your eyes, or concentrate on a pretty picture on your wall or your computer screen. Like the other locations, you can set an intention, ask a question, or simply focus on clearing your mind.

Depending on how your day is going, if you are feeling stressed, setting an intention is great because it distracts your mind from the negative feelings stress causes. Repeating an affirmation will help block out those negative stressors to keep you going the rest of the day. If you are in overwhelm mode, focusing on clearing out your mind and intentionally thinking about a blank space or your third eye helps knock out all those thoughts twisting in your head.

When we are in overwhelm it's usually because we have way too many thoughts we are focusing on at once. The act of concentrating on clearing our minds stops that wheel in our heads from turning. That in turn breaks the cycle of all those thoughts so we can stop, focus, and concentrate on our priorities.

On the treadmill

If it's cold or stormy outside and you prefer the walking meditation, do it on your treadmill! You can set the mood by listening to tranquil music and focusing on a pleasing object in the room (or bring one along if you're doing this at your gym.)

I would not recommend closing your eyes as that would be a potential hazard, but concentrating on a pleasant object like serene artwork or a picture that brings you joy helps during the times that you can't be outside but you'd like to keep moving.

Take a class

If you like to be surrounded by others or like to be instructed on what to do, classes are a fun and beneficial way to either start out or take your meditation game to the next level. This is especially great for the tai chi option since there are actual synchronized motions involved.

I have a lot of fun going to meditation classes because I don't have the same experience every time. There is always something new or different that is brought to the class. The instructor is also a great source to keep your intentions on the right track. If your mind keeps drifting at home while you meditate, are bored, or would just like to see how a meditation class feels, go try one out! That compounded optimism of others in the same room intentionally focusing on serenity makes the tranquility palpable!

Give as many of these locations a try as you'd like, and if you found your favorite don't forget you can always mix it up to staunch the mundane from your practice.

The great thing about meditation practice is that you don't have to be a pro and there is no perfect way to do it. This is a *practice* for the beginner as well as the professional. We will get different results every time we sit down. The importance is that we continue to show up so that the time spent outside of the practice is more tranquil, and adversities have less of an affect on us.

Chapter 5: Setting the Stage

Prepare yourself. Before you begin, figure out which meditation practice you'd like to try, where you'd like to do it, and set the mood. Setting the mood is as important as the actual practice. You wouldn't try to sleep while you have the lights on, the blender running, and the tv on at the same time. You take a shower, put your pajamas right, make sure the doors are locked and the lights are out, and that the kids are sleeping. Then you make sure you have your blankets and your pillows, and you turn out the lights.

The same intentions go for meditation. After you pick where you are going to meditate, set the mood. If you are in a room, light some candles and put on some serene music. Wear some comfortable clothes. If you are at the office, put on your headphones to listen to your tranquil music, and have a pleasant spot to focus on if you'd like to keep your eyes open. If you are sitting or lying on the ground, use some pillows or a yoga mat so you are more comfortable. If you are going to a park, make sure it's one that you find is serene.

You can set a timer while you meditate so you don't have to keep thinking about the time. It is essential though that you meditate for the time you've decided to in order to affirm that you are taking your meditation as seriously as you do brushing your teeth. If you set a timer and after a while think things like "I can just stop now. I think I've finished for the day." Once you start to convince yourself that cutting corners is okay, you'll start to meditate less and less each day, and will eventually stop altogether. So, make sure you set a realistic time, and stick with it to get the amazing results meditation can bring to your life!

Make sure to remove all distractions such as loud noises, children, etc. If possible. If your phone is on, turn it on vibrate or put it in another room. Turn off the tv unless you are listening to something soothing on it. Close your windows if you live in a high-traffic area. Go to a place where you are alone and feel comfortable.

Your meditation practice is your time, and even though you are only spending a little bit of time during your day to practice it, if you want to gain the benefits, put in the effort to ensure you are going to get the intended advantages. Making sure there is nothing to distract you while your mind is in this wonderful healing process ensures its success.

Chapter 6: Get Your Body Involved

You've got your location, you've set your atmosphere and your timer. The next thing to think about is what your body is saying.

Relax everything: A highly successful and relaxing technique is to concentrate relaxing each part of your body one at a time, from head to toe, throughout the whole meditation session. Start from your toes, up to your calves, to your knees, then your bottom, your stomach, up to your heart, your shoulders, down your arms, to your fingers, then up to your neck, and to the top of your head. Relax your jaw, your mouth, your eyes, your lips. Focusing on each body part has two results: It makes you relax the parts you never even knew you were clenching, and it also stops you from thinking about anything else, which is kind of the point of meditation.

If you are sitting, make sure you are in a comfortable position. You can sit in a cross-legged position. If there is any knee pain, you can put pillows under your knees. Make sure your bottom is well padded, because if it's not, you'll be focusing on that your entire practice and not toward your intention. If you are flexible you can be in the lotus pose (where your feet are pulled up and resting above your legs, the soles of your feet against your stomach.) Just know if you are feeling any discomfort feel free to adjust accordingly. You can sit up straight in the middle of the room, or your can rest your back against a wall or cushion. With a sitting meditation, make sure there are no kinks in any body parts. You want your intentions to flow freely throughout your body.

If you are walking, make sure you are wearing comfortable shoes so your feet aren't a distraction. The focus here is to relax your shoulders and your neck. We tend to carry a lot of tension in our shoulders and neck, so taking this time to relax them is an added bonus. Swaying your arms from side to side is also a soothing method of concentration. Keeping your core connected will also help your body to align with your intentions.

If you are laying down, lie on something comfortable. If you are lying on your back, have some space between your feet, as well as your hands from your sides. Take up as much room as you want. I like to take up a LOT of room when I am lying on the ground. This makes me feel the most relaxed. If that is just too much space, you can have your feet hip-width apart and your arms the just a little out from your sides.

If you are lying on your side, you can get into fetal position, where your knees are stacked on top of each other and bent up toward your stomach to relax your spine. Your hands can be resting under your head.

The intention of lying meditation is to relax everything, so taking mental inventory of every body part while in this position is beneficial.

Whether walking or lying down, it's clear that the main focus is to keep reminding yourself to relax. And being comfortable ensures you aren't getting distracted from your intentions while you meditate. We want to be relaxed and comfortable while we meditate so we can connect our body's intention with our mind's to heighten our results from our practice.

Chapter 7: Take a Breath

Do you ever notice when we are going through something extremely difficult, like an anxiety attack, or overcoming a fear, or we are in labor, people tell us to focus on breathing? This is because breathing actually helps our minds overcome obstacles. The same goes when you meditate. Holding your breath when you meditate stops your intentions to reaching through your entire body and out to the world. It can also slow your mental thoughts because you're not getting as much oxygen into your brain as is needed.

Becoming more open to being present in the moment

by the simple act of consciously being mindful of your breath creates an incredible inner restoration.

Breath is crucial to meditation. It is the fuel for our brain and our body, and to break that flow is detrimental physically and mentally. During the entire meditation practice, focus on breathing in and out so as not to hold your breath.

Breathe in. Breathe out. Breathe in and focus on something that makes you happy. Then breathe out as you focus on the negative issues that are cramming your head. Then repeat: Breathe in to bring in the positive. Breathe out to empty out the negative. You can keep doing this until you are satisfied that you have cleared your mind, or you can do this the entire practice. I've done this many times, and it is actually one of my favorite types of meditation practices.

When we breathe in, we are inhaling the clean air that our bodies need, and when we exhale, our bodies are getting rid of the bad air that our bodies are over and done with. It makes sense then, that to clear our minds we inhale cleansing thoughts and exhale the toxic ones. It helps restore our minds right alongside our bodies.

When we hold our breath, it stops the natural flow of our bodies from our blood flow to our chemical balance. When you inhale, imagine your breath filling up all the places in your body: your heart, your head, your thighs, your fingers, your toes. When you exhale, imagine all the negative events being exhaled out too. Exhale all the way until you have nothing left.

You may be wondering why we are covering breath so

much. I mean, we all breathe throughout our day in order to survive. But the truth is, when we are stressed, overwhelmed, scared, we hold our breath. So if we live a stressful life, we are regularly stifling our oxygen flow on a daily basis. This only compounds our issues.

The more you concentrate on breath in your meditation practice, the more your body will intentionally know to do so during the rest of the day when you are not mediating. Which means when you are faced with an adverse moment, your mind tells you to breathe (thanks meditation!) and you overcome that obstacle more quickly than you would have before.

Chapter 8: Clear Your Mind

You're ready to start your meditation. You've set the scene, lit the candles, gotten comfortable, released you tension in your body, set your intention, and you're breathing. You've closed your eyes to focus.

And you can't seem to concentrate. Your head is filled with all the things you need to get done before the end of the day. You're thinking about Karen who stole your yogurt in the breakroom but completely denied it. You're thinking about your fight with your mother. You're worried you about what you're going to do about your money problems.

We've got so much to stress over. Every day there is plenty of negative things going on in our lives that take over our thoughts. And a daily meditation practice is the best solution to help us ease this stress by actively ending the stress-ridden conversation in our heads. But what do we do when we sit down and can't seem to concentrate on emptying our minds? What do we do when we can't seem to stop concentrating on that which we'd like not to?

If you find your mind drifting off to things you don't want to think about, realize it, recognize it, and go back to concentrating on what brings you contentment. And know that this happens to everyone. It's important not to get upset or frustrated with yourself over this. It is all part of the beautiful experience of the practice.

Close your eyes and concentrate on the darkness behind them. Focus on that dark area and every time an unwanted thought pops into your head, acknowledge that it's happening, and let it drift off. You can even imagine this thought being scooped up into a bubble, floating away and popping in the distance. This is a more concentrated method of letting distracting thoughts go.

Another option when we are trying to clear our minds and think of nothing is when our eyes are closed to concentrate on your "third eye" which is the location just above and between your eyebrows. This is where a lot of people's personal centers are and one of my personal favorite places to concentrate on when meditating. I find that when I concentrate on it I'm more connected to nature and living things all around me.

You can also concentrate on a picture in your mind. What scene do you think about when you are stressed and want to get away from a situation? Do you picture yourself on a beach with crashing waves in front of you and a nice breeze on your skin? Do you find yourself in front of a gorgeous waterfall in the middle of the jungle? How about kayaking on a beautiful lake while a sea turtle swims alongside you? This can be a very powerful option when you just can't seem to clear your head.

If you prefer to have your eyes open, you can focus on a burning candle, or a picture or decoration on your wall, or even a nice blank wall. You can experiment with the objects until you've found the one that brings you the most tranquility.

You are learning how to clear your mind. Learning comes with bumps in the road. And those bumps are what makes you a stronger person. So, the next time you are distracted, simply re-focus your mind, and see your meditation practice through to its end. And if you don't concentrate during the entire practice, try again the next day.

There's no need to focus on the fact that you couldn't concentrate. Just recognize it and attempt it again. It's as simple as that. Part of the meditation results is not being negatively affected by adverse situations, which includes what happens during the meditation practice. So, don't be discouraged if you can't seem to concentrate when just starting out, and don't get dispirited if all the sudden you can't concentrate after days of success. This happens to everyone—even the professional meditators. Keep coming back, keep practicing, and you will feel the results. And your mind will thank you!

Chapter 9: Aim True

Why are we not meditating? Many people lead highly stressful lives that are jam-packed with countless chores, commitments, errands, and meetings. How do we even begin to find the time to fit a new practice in? The truth is meditation can take as little as five minutes a day. If you can get up five minutes earlier, or take five minutes of your lunch break, or spend five glorious minutes laying on your bed with a candle lit to practice meditation, it will sneak into your routine in no time.

And what if you forget to meditate? Try again the next

day. Like any good habit we attempt to begin, we won't get further by making ourselves feel bad for not doing it. Just do it the next day. It's that simple. We don't have to spend any more time worrying about the fact that we forgot than the simple split-second decision to just do it.

The second thing that stops us from meditating is finding justification in our excuses. There are so many fun activities at the beginning of our days, like sleeping in. And at the end of our day, we have distracting instant gratifications like snacks and tv.

Wanting to feel good in the moment is such a strong emotion that it's so easy to convince ourselves to do it. But it isn't what we need in the long run. If you can stop in that moment you decide between eating Oreos and working out, and think about which one will actually benefit you, you'll be more able to make the more life-enhancing choice.

I had to make my own affirmation for this. Whenever I was feeling tired or wanted something to make me feel better in the moment, I started reciting one simple statement "This decision will or won't benefit the future me." That is all it took for me. This mantra can help you if you struggle with the same instant gratification mindset most of us have developed, or you can create your own that is more specific and powerful for the habits you're trying to do away with.

Affirmations are very popular to use during a meditation. These are words or sentences you can repeat over and over in your meditation to bring positive thoughts in. Some examples are "love," or "peace," or "I am freaking amazing."

Affirmations can be of your own creation. The important thing is that it is something that makes you feel positive, and that resonates with you. If you're sitting there the entire practice thinking about the word "butterflies" when you could really care less about butterflies, pick another affirmation.

My affirmations of choice usually differ from day to day depending on whatever particularly vivid spectacle life has in store for me, but some of my personal favorites are: "Love flows in and out of me," "I am in harmony with my highest self," and "fuck that shit" to name just a few. Repeat as you inhale and exhale. You can also have one affirmation while you inhale, then another as you exhale.

Affirmations will be most important when you start a regular meditation practice to help you focus, but focusing will get easier as time goes on, because again, meditating makes us more grounded and able to stay in the moment.

Did you know the more you focus on something and the more emotions you feel around it, the more you create those emotions? That's why when you are meditating and you are quieting your mind and focusing, the more important it is that you concentrate on something that makes you calm and happy. If you are meditating with your eyes open, concentrate on something that is soothing. This can be a pleasant picture, a lit candle, a calming color on a wall, a decoration. Just make sure the feelings you are having while you look at it are positive.

What would you like to focus on? Do you have a specific question you would like to ask the universe? Or do you have too much in your head and would like to focus on clearing your mind? Do you have an affirmation you would like to focus on? Setting your intentions prior to your meditation helps keep you focused. Which is beneficial since you might not be meditating for very long.

Stay in the moment. During your allotted meditation time, your only goal is to stay with your intention you set. If you have a question, focus on that. You can also focus on your breathing. You can focus on your affirmations, your candle, relaxing your body, and all of the other things associated in settling you in your meditation. Don't focus on the time, or what you're going to make for dinner, or all of the things you need to do tomorrow. Just focus on your moment and your intention. That is how your mind relaxes.

Chapter 10: Persistence is Key

If you have never meditated before, or have given it a try once or twice in your lifetime, you'll probably wonder when you'll know you're doing it right? The answer is simple. Try, and you're doing it right.

It's called a meditation practice for a reason. Meditation can have a different effect every time. The point is to come back every day to attempt to clear your head and focus on positive thoughts. Just the attempt to meditate daily is where the important work gets done. The fact that you are setting your daily meditation routine helps build confidence and establishes a positive accord with yourself.

If at times you are in your meditation practice, and are really trying to focus on your intensions and are just not succeeding, it's important to understand that that's not the point. It's the fact that you have set the intention to meditate. Even though sometimes you won't succeed, more often than not you will. And as you gradually build your practice, you'll be more successful in your intentions.

You will also start to notice that you are focusing on your intentions, but you might be thinking that it isn't working. When we begin a meditation practice, we aren't yet attuned to its benefits until we start to notice throughout our regular routine of work, chores, and errands that our normal daily life will be more peaceful.

You'll feel happier, and the stressors that once bothered you will begin to affect you less and less. And as you continue to practice, you'll notice a lasting effect on your outlook and demeanor. So, just because at the beginning it may be hard to focus while you sit there, and you may not notice any effects meditation is having on you in the beginning, the important part is to stick with it.

It's much like exercising. We all know it's good for us and that we won't see the effects right away, but we also know that the more we stick with our workout routine, the more we will see the results. So, stick with it. Keep coming back every day. It's only five minutes out of your day. And after a while you will start to see the benefits.

Realize that every day will be blissfully different
No one knows why, but our bodies are changing from day to day. People who constantly work their bodies by stretching, working out, and physical labor understand what I'm talking about. For instance, even when a really flexible person stretches their legs every day, some days they'll be able to touch their nose to their knee caps, and the next day they won't be able to. Then the next day they will. There is a wonderful discussion that is going on with all our body parts every day, so it is constantly changing on the tiniest scale.

The same thing goes with how your body and mind will react to meditation. You can be meditating for months with success every day, then all the sudden one day you can't seem to concentrate. Or you don't feel like doing the same meditation practice you've been doing. Or your body doesn't want to be in the same position you're normally in during your practice. Or you'd like to mix up your routine. Or you don't feel like closing your eyes. Or you'd rather be outside because it's a beautiful day.

The wonderful thing about taking care of your mind and body is that you don't have to hold yourself to the exact workout you've established. If you'd like to mix it up, try a different practice. Try meditating outside on a beautiful day. Try laying down if your body is just not comfortable sitting. Open your eyes if you don't want to keep them closed. If you've worked up to 20 minutes daily and you just want to do five minutes, do five minutes. It's completely up to you. Just keep coming back.

Conclusion

The benefits of meditation are so great it's a wonder it isn't discussed as much as dieting and exercise. When we think about it, our minds need as much love and rest as our bodies do. And meditation is so simple. All it takes is just five minutes a day and the rest of our time will be more tranquil, difficulties will affect us less, we'll be less stressed, we wont have as much anxiety, we will understand others more; the list of benefits is endless.

Adding a meditation practice to your daily routine will help you face any obstacles that come your way. You'll look forward to your day, and you'll learn to find the beauty in each moment throughout each day.

All you have to do is show up every day. Something this important that basically takes no time at all should be as non-negotiable to your routine as drinking water. It is so beneficial, yet so simple that we don't think about it as much as we should.

I personally sometimes forget to meditate, but I can slowly feel the consequences the longer I don't do it. I start to feel more stressed and hopeless, and short tempered, and sluggish and tired. So set reminders on your phone or put a pretty sticky note on your bathroom mirror.

Get in the habit of doing it every day.

So have fun with your meditation practice. Mix it up, try new meditation practices. Set the stage where you plan to meditate so your ambience can match your intention. Light candles. Concentrate on something that gives you inner peace. Set your timer so you can focus on more important things than whether or not your time is up. Dress in comfortable clothes. Mix up your practice so you don't get bored. Just keep trying every day. Because Every time counts.

Remember that it is a practice for a reason. You may find certain days harder to concentrate that others. You also will experience extremely profound days where you actually feel overwhelming fits of giddiness that are incredible and are unlike anything you've experienced. But the fact that you are practicing is the point. Keep showing up. The results may change from day to day during your meditation, the benefits will only grow. The act of meditating makes the time spent outside of your practice heavenly.

Stick with it. Show up and practice meditating every day and over time you'll feel like you can handle anything. Because you truly can.